THE AMERICAN QUARTER HORSE

By Ellen Frazel

Consultant:
Dr. Emily Leuthner
DVM, MS, DACVIM
Country View Veterinary Service
Oregon, Wisc.

BELLWETHER MEDIA • MINNEAPOLIS, MN

Jump into the cockpit and take flight with *Pilot Books*. Your journey will take you on high-energy adventures as you learn about all that is wild, weird, fascinating, and fun!

This edition first published in 2012 by Bellwether Media, Inc.

No part of this publication may be reproduced in whole or in part without written permission of the publisher. For information regarding permission, write to Bellwether Media, Inc., Attention: Permissions Department, 5357 Penn Avenue South, Minneapolis, MN 55419.

Library of Congress Cataloging-in-Publication Data

Frazel, Ellen.
 The American quarter horse / by Ellen Frazel.
   p. cm. – (Pilot books. Horse breed roundup)
 Includes bibliographical references and index.
 Summary: "Engaging images accompany information about the American Quarter Horse. The combination of high-interest subject matter and narrative text is intended for students in grades 3 through 7"–Provided by publisher.
 ISBN 978-1-60014-653-4 (hardcover : alk. paper)
 1. Quarter horse–Juvenile literature. I. Title.
SF293.Q3F73 2012
636.1'33–dc22   2011010411

Printed in the United States of America, North Mankato, MN.

080111   1187

CONTENTS

The American Quarter Horse

The excitement of a horse race is in the air. The crowd cheers as the horses wait behind the gates. Suddenly, the loud crack of a gunshot sounds. The horses are off! Their hooves pound the dirt as they speed by the stands. The horses complete the quarter-mile track in less than 25 seconds. It is a **photo finish**. The judges need a second look to determine the winner. It is an American Quarter Horse!

The American Quarter Horse was named for its ability to run a quarter mile in record time. The horse is a skilled sprinter. It is the most popular horse breed in the United States. People across the country enjoy playing and working with this strong, **agile**, and intelligent breed.

How Fast?
American Quarter Horses
are nicknamed
"the world's fastest athletes."

American Quarter Horses get their speed from their strong, muscular bodies. They have very powerful **hindquarters**. The horses are known for their small heads, little ears, and short manes. Their sleek coats come in 17 different colors. The most common coat color is a brownish red called sorrel. Other coat colors include gray, **blue roan**, black, **palomino**, and chestnut. The American Quarter Horse's **temperament** is energetic and pleasant.

The breed has four different body types. Stock horses work on ranches where they herd cattle and do other tasks. They are the shortest type of American Quarter Horse, but they are strong and quick. Halter horses are taller and very muscular. They compete in horse shows where they are judged on how well they represent the breed. The racing type has long legs to sprint short distances. The show hunter is slimmer so it can leap over fences and hurdles in competitions.

An Early Racer

A mix of a few powerful horse breeds produced the American Quarter Horse. The story starts in the early American **colonies**, where farmers liked to race their horses for fun. The farmers wanted faster horses than the ones they had brought with them from England. In the early 1600s, the colonists began to trade horses with a Native American tribe called the Chickasaw. This tribe gave the colonists horses called Spanish Barbs.

In Search of Gold

In the 1500s, famous Spanish explorers including Hernán Cortés and Francisco Vásquez de Coronado rode Spanish Barbs as they roamed the Americas in search of gold.

Spanish Barb

In 1611, Spanish Barbs were bred with the English horses of the colonists. The result was a new, faster breed of horse. These horses entertained the colonists over the next 150 years. People gathered on the main streets of villages throughout the colonies. They watched as the horses blazed their way down quarter-mile stretches. People began calling the breed "The Celebrated American Quarter Running Horse."

In the early 1700s, a horse named the Godolphin Arabian changed horse racing forever. He **sired** Janus, one of the first thoroughbreds. In 1752, Janus was brought from England to the American Colonies. A man named John Randolph bred Janus with colonial racing horses. The **offspring** were early versions of the modern American Quarter Horse.

Around this time, the Thoroughbred became the favorite racing horse in the colonies. However, American Quarter Horses still had an important purpose. Their small, sturdy build made them perfect for exploring the **frontier**. Over time, people brought them into the American West. There, a **foal** named Sir Archy was born in 1805.

the Godolphin Arabian

The last horses to contribute to the American Quarter Horse were the Spanish Mustangs used by the Native Americans in the West. These horses were related to the Spanish Barbs. The **descendants** of Janus and Sir Archy were bred with these tough, fast horses.

In 1844, a descendant of Sir Archy named Steel Dust came to Texas. He is one of the most famous **foundation horses** of the American Quarter Horse breed. Steel Dust was also a racing champion. His legend spread as cowboys used his offspring for **cattle drives** from Texas to the Great Plains. Strong and intelligent, these fast horses were the first of the modern American Quarter Horse breed.

Rodeos, Ranches, and Racing

The American Quarter Horse Association (AQHA) **registers** American Quarter Horses. It began in Texas in 1940. Today, more than 4 million registered American Quarter Horses live in the United States. American Quarter Horses are used in **rodeos**, competitions, and races. They are also popular workhorses on ranches.

American Quarter Horses are very good at speed events called **gymkhana**. These events highlight the American Quarter Horse's ability to perform quick, precise movements. Many events require good teamwork between riders and horses. American Quarter Horses succeed at gymkhana because of their intelligence and agility.

In a gymkhana event called barrel racing, a horse and rider try to weave around three barrels at top speed. The barrels are spaced in a triangle and are between 60 and 105 feet (18 and 32 meters) apart. The horse and rider must hug the outlines of the barrels. The closer they get to the barrels, the faster they can get around them!

American Quarter Horses also compete in rodeo events such as calf roping. In this event, a horse and rider chase after a calf. The goal is to throw a rope around the neck and then tie up its legs. The horse and rider start behind a barrier. The calf runs out of a chute, getting a head start. Then the barrier opens and the horse is released. The chase is on!

Cowboy Speeding Ticket

In calf roping, riders often put their horses into a gallop behind the barrier. A rider can get a penalty called a "Cowboy Speeding Ticket" if he or she crosses the barrier too soon.

Calling All Cowgirls!

More women than men compete in barrel racing. In 2010, Sherry Cervi set a record of completing a barrel race course in only 13.49 seconds!

Famous American Quarter Horses

Chicks Beduino

Chicks Beduino

Chicks Beduino was born in 1984. By 2006, his offspring had won so many races that he became second on the list of all-time most famous American Quarter Horse sires.

Evening Snow

Sired by Chicks Beduino, Evening Snow was born in 1993. In 1996, he became the first horse of any breed to run a quarter-mile race in under 21 seconds. He clocked in at 20.94 seconds.

Whosleavingwho

Also sired by Chicks Beduino, Whosleavingwho was born in 1998. He is known for sharing the World Champion title with Streakin Sin Tacha in 2002. In 2003, Whosleavingwho recorded the third-fastest time ever in the quarter-mile race. He completed the track in 19.38 seconds!

American Quarter Horses are still used by ranchers to herd and drive cattle. They also compete in different events at western riding competitions. In reining competitions, they try to complete a series of circles, spins, and other movements at the command of their riders. Their experience following orders on ranches often helps them win.

The American Quarter Horse will always be famous for its speed. Sprinting down the straightaway past a crowd of fans has been a part of its history for hundreds of years. Today, the American Quarter Horse can run as fast as 55 miles (88.5 kilometers) per hour. The quarter mile is in its blood, and the blood of this breed has never stopped pounding!

Glossary

agile—able to move the body quickly and with ease

blue roan—a coat with a black base color and white hairs; this makes the coat look blue.

cattle drives—the moving of large groups of cattle from one place to another

colonies—early settlements in a new land by people from another country

descendants—younger family members who all come from an older family member

foal—a young horse; foals are under one year old.

foundation horses—the first horses of a specific breed; all horses of a breed can trace their bloodlines back to the foundation horses.

frontier—unexplored wilderness on the edge of settled land; the West was the great frontier of the United States in the 1800s.

gymkhana—horse events that involve speed pattern racing; barrel racing is a gymkhana event.

hindquarters—the hind legs and muscles of a four-legged animal

offspring—an animal's young

palomino—a gold coat, usually with a white mane or tail

photo finish—when a race is so close that judges must look at a video to determine the winner

registers—makes record of; owners register their horses with official breed organizations.

rodeos—competitions in which riders perform various skills on horses

sired—fathered

temperament—personality or nature; the American Quarter Horse has an energetic, pleasant temperament.

To Learn More

At the Library

Dell, Pamela. *American Quarter Horses.* Chanhassen, Minn.: Child's World, 2007.

Price, Steven D. *The Kids' Book of the American Quarter Horse.* New York, N.Y.: Lyons Press, 1999.

Stone, Lynn M. *American Quarter Horses.* Vero Beach, Fla.: Rourke Pub., 2008.

On the Web

Learning more about American Quarter Horses is as easy as 1, 2, 3.

1. Go to www.factsurfer.com.

2. Enter "American Quarter Horses" into the search box.

3. Click the "Surf" button and you will see a list of related Web sites.

With factsurfer.com, finding more information is just a click away.

Index

The images in this book are reproduced through the courtesy of: Juniors Bildarchiv / Photolibrary, front cover; Lincoln Rogers, pp. 4-5; Ellwood Eppard, pp. 6, 11; Frank Lukasseck / Getty Images, p. 7; Buddy Mays / Alamy, p. 8; imagebroker / Age Fotostock, p. 9; Public Domain, pp. 10, 18 (small); Daisy Gillardini / Getty Images, pp. 12-13; Cindy Farr-Weinfeld, pp. 14-15; Christopher Halloran, pp. 16-17; Juniors Bildarchiv / Age Fotostock, pp. 18-19; Mark J. Barrett / Alamy, pp. 20-21.